My First Book of Biographies

My First Book

Great Men and Women

# of Biographies

Every Child Should Know

by Jean Marzollo
Illustrated by Irene Trivas

Cartwheel
·B·O·O·K·S·®
SCHOLASTIC INC.
New York Toronto London Auckland Sydney

For Sheila and Ru Rauch
—J.M.

For Grace Rebecca Cade
—I.T.

With thanks to Carolyn Yoder of *Cobblestone* magazine,
Ru Rauch, Kristin O'Connell, and Barry O'Connell,
for generous and perceptive advice.

ISBN 0-590-45015-8

12 11 10 9 8 7 6 5 4 3 2   8 9/9 0 1 2/0

Printed in the U.S.A.

Introduction

The stories of famous people show us that girls and boys of all cultures and backgrounds can grow up to be powerful adults. The 45 historical figures in this book come from different times in history and different kinds of families. Some were wealthy; many were poor. What do they have in common? As you will see, they were passionate about their work. They worked hard, and they took risks to accomplish their goals.

These 45 people are only a fraction of the many great people who have influenced our world. We apologize if we left your favorite historical heroes and heroines out of this book; they're probably on our list for the next one.

Please keep in mind that the biographies, presented alphabetically, are meant only to introduce you to these folks. Hopefully, you'll find them so interesting that you'll want to read more about them now and as you grow. Your school and public libraries contain biographies on all levels — from picture books to easy-to-read books to young adult and adult books.

Because the introductory biographies in this book are short, not every fact can be included and not every word is explained. If you need to know something, ask someone to help you find the information in your library. Libraries are filled with books containing interesting facts and opinions.

If you come across a word you don't understand, look it up in a dictionary or ask a grown-up, "What does this mean?" Encourage the voice within yourself that asks questions and seeks answers.

Jean Marzollo, author
Irene Trivas, illustrator

Table of Contents

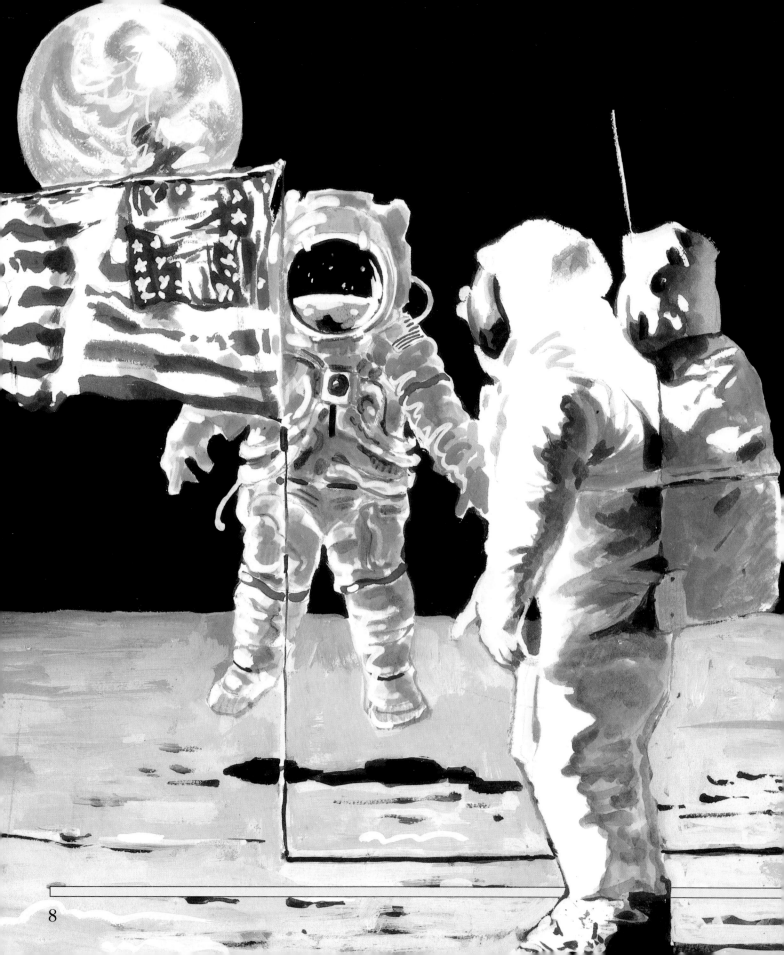

Neil Armstrong (1930–)
Edwin Aldrin, Jr. (1930–)

They were the first people to walk on the moon.

For many years, people gazed at the moon and dreamed of a day when they might be able to travel there in a spaceship. The dream seemed impossible until 1957. That year, the Soviet Union (now split into Russia and other countries) sent the satellite Sputnik into space. A year later, the U.S. government started the National Aeronautics and Space Administration (NASA). NASA hired scientists, engineers, factory workers, and pilots called astronauts. The word astronaut means "sailor in the stars."

The early 1960's were exciting. The Soviet Union and the United States raced to see who could accomplish the most in space. In 1969, the United States sent the Apollo 11 lunar module 238,000 miles away to the moon. People on earth watched on TV as astronaut Neil Armstrong climbed down from the spacecraft. He was the first person to set foot on the moon. People heard him say, "That's one small step for a man and one giant leap for mankind."

Astronaut Edwin Aldrin, Jr., followed 18 minutes later. The two astronauts planted a flag on the moon. Walking on the moon felt odd because there is little gravity there. Gravity is a force that pulls people to the ground. Because there is less gravity on the moon than on Earth, the astronauts bounced when they walked.

Because there is no air on the moon, they breathed air from tanks on their backs. They spoke to each other through radios. On the moon the astronauts found a hard surface covered with rocky soil. There were no animals, no plants, no air, no wind, and no water. Neil Armstrong and Edwin Aldrin, Jr., took some of the soil back to Earth for scientists to study.

Neil Armstrong and Edwin Aldrin, Jr., took photographs of the moon. They also took photos of Earth from their spacecraft. They said that from far away Earth looks like a big blue marble.

Rachel Carson (1907–1964)

In her books, she told people to care for the earth.

When Rachel Carson was a young girl in Springdale, Pennsylvania, she liked to read and write. At the age of ten, she sold a story she had written to a magazine for ten dollars.

Rachel was also interested in plants and animals. She studied these subjects in college and afterwards in graduate school. Because Rachel did so well, she received scholarships to pay for her studies. When she was finished, she had to choose. What should she be—a writer or a scientist? Rachel Carson decided to be both.

She wrote about plants and animals for the United States Fish and Wildlife Service. She also published several books about nature. In *The Sea Around Us*, Rachel Carson helped people learn about the ocean. Many people bought this book.

Her last book, *Silent Spring*, was published in 1962. In it, Rachel Carson warned people not to spray pesticides, or bug killers, on the earth. These pesticides, such as DDT, were supposed to kill only harmful insects. But they also were killing helpful insects, as well as birds and fish. Rachel Carson warned that some animals might become extinct because of DDT. Extinct means that the animals would no longer exist.

She said pesticides could harm humans, too. *Silent Spring* changed the way people thought about nature. Most people had not worried about air and water before. Now they began to feel responsible for keeping the environment clean and healthy. They began to take action, too. For example, lawmakers passed a law saying that DDT could no longer be used.

Rachel Carson's choice to write about animals and plants made the world a better place for all living things.

George Washington Carver (c. 1864–1943)

He discovered hundreds of new uses for plants.

George Washington Carver was born a slave in Diamond, Missouri. A slave is a person who is owned by someone else. The owner can make the slave work for no pay. In the early history of the United States, white people in the South brought black people from Africa and forced them to work on their farms. When these slaves had children, their birth dates were not always written down. That is why there is a *c* before the date above. It stands for *circa* (SER-ka), which means "about." George Washington Carver was born about 1864.

Shortly after he was born, his father was killed in an accident and his mother was kidnapped. George was raised by his owners. In 1865, when George was one year old and Abraham Lincoln was president, slavery was abolished, or ended. The people who had owned George continued to raise him. They taught him to read and write.

As a child, George loved plants. When he grew up, he went to college and studied agriculture, the science of farming. It was very hard for African Americans to go to college then because many colleges did not accept black people. George Washington Carver worked at different jobs to pay for his education. When he was 32, he was asked to teach at the Tuskegee Institute, a college for African Americans. He taught agricultural students how to grow more plants on their land.

Although he liked teaching, George Washington Carver liked scientific research more. He liked to look at plants and ask, "What would happen if . . . ?" George Washington Carver experimented with peanuts, sweet potatoes, and soybeans in his laboratory. He discovered more than 300 different products, including ink, soap, and a milk substitute that could be made from peanuts alone.

George Washington Carver was given many prizes for his research. Toward the end of his life, Carver gave much of the money he had earned to the Tuskegee Institute, so that other scientists could work and study there, too.

Peanut Milk

Peanut Ink

Peanut Soap

NFWA

AFL-CIO

NFWA

HUELGA

14

Cesar Chavez (1927–1993)

He helped migrant farm workers.

Cesar Chavez lived the first ten years of his life on a small farm near Yuma, Arizona. His family and most of the Mexican American families around him spoke Spanish. Many were farm families who grew their own food on their own land. Because these people were poor, they couldn't pay their taxes—so the government took their land away from them. Many of them moved to California to become migrant farm workers. Migrant workers travel from farm to farm picking fruits and vegetables when they are ripe.

Cesar Chavez was ten years old when his family moved to California. Migrant work was hard. His family and the other migrant families lived in shacks with no running water. The workers spoke Spanish; the farm owners spoke English. It was hard for the workers to discuss problems with the owners, who often didn't want to hear about them. Some children of migrant workers worked in the fields and received no schooling. Others had to keep changing schools. By the time Cesar was in eighth grade, he had gone to more than 30 schools. Despite this, he learned to speak and read English.

When Cesar Chavez grew up, he became a leader of the migrant workers. He helped them learn to read and to vote. He helped them form a union called the National Farm Workers' Association (NFWA). The NFWA was later called the UFW (for United Farm Workers). In 1965, grape workers went on strike—*huelga* in Spanish. A strike is a refusal to do something until certain people do what you want. In this case, the workers refused to work until the farmers recognized their right to a union and fair pay. Cesar Chavez and the union asked people across the United States to support the strike by boycotting, or not buying, grapes. Through strikes and boycotts, Cesar Chavez helped migrant workers gain better housing, higher pay, more schooling, and respect for their union.

Winston Churchill (1874–1965)

He helped save England from Hitler's Nazis.

As a young boy, Winston Churchill did poorly in school. His parents and teachers were sure he would never do well, but young Winston surprised them. He grew up to be the prime minister of England during World War II. The prime minister of England is the chief government leader in the country, much like the president of the United States.

During World War II, England was attacked by Nazi Germany under its dictator, Adolf Hitler. Hitler wanted to conquer many countries. He had already taken over Poland, Denmark, Norway, France, and Holland. England was next. Under Winston Churchill, however, the English fought back.

There was no television back then. Winston Churchill spoke to his people on the radio. He wrote his own speeches, and they were magnificent. His words helped the English people feel brave. "We shall fight on the beaches," he said. "We shall fight on the landing grounds, we shall fight in the fields and in the streets, we shall fight in the hills: We shall never surrender."

When German pilots dropped bombs on London, Winston Churchill visited frightened people in factories, stores, and homes. He held up his fingers in a V-for-Victory sign to show them that he wasn't afraid. When English planes shot down Nazi planes, Winston Churchill praised the pilots for their bravery. "Never," he said, "in the field of human conflict was so much owed by so many to so few."

He asked the English people to fight hard. "Let us therefore brace ourselves to our duties," he said, "and so bear ourselves that if the British Empire and its Commonwealth last for a thousand years, men will still say, 'This was their finest hour.'"

And what a fine hour it was! In 1945, England (along with the United States and other Allied countries) defeated Nazi Germany (and Japan) to win World War II.

Cleopatra (69–30 B.C.)

She was queen of ancient Egypt.

Cleopatra became queen of ancient Egypt in 51 B.C. (B.C. means *before Christ*. The years before the birth of Jesus are counted backwards from 1.) When Cleopatra became queen, she was eighteen years old. Her throne was in Alexandria, a splendid city. For a while her younger brother, who was ten, ruled with her. But his advisers wanted him to have all the power. Cleopatra and her brother became enemies. Cleopatra left Alexandria and began to gather an army for war.

Cleopatra heard that the Roman leader, Julius Caesar, was visiting Alexandria. She wanted to ask him to help her, but she didn't know how to meet him without her enemies finding out. It is said that she had an aide wrap her in a rug and sneak her into Caesar's private quarters.

Caesar was impressed with Cleopatra and fell in love with her. He helped her win back the Egyptian throne and become Egypt's queen again.

Caesar lived with Cleopatra in Alexandria; then she lived with him for two years in Rome. When he was killed in 44 B.C., Cleopatra returned to Egypt and ruled her country. She restored the war-damaged Alexandrian Library, which contained famous ancient scrolls. She also invited scholars from around the world to visit her city.

At this time, a leader named Mark Antony was gaining power in Rome. In 41 B.C., he invited Queen Cleopatra to visit. Cleopatra sailed to see Antony with a fleet of twelve ships. She wore her most splendid robes, and her ship was lit with burning torches. Antony also fell in love with Cleopatra. He gave her Roman books to add to her library and married her in 37 B.C.

Many stories and plays have been written about Antony and Cleopatra. The most famous play is *Antony and Cleopatra* by William Shakespeare.

Christopher Columbus (1451–1506)

He was a brave sailor and great explorer.

Christopher Columbus lived about five hundred years ago. At the time, people in European countries, such as France and Spain, bought spices and other goods from the Indies. The Indies was what they called India, China, the East Indies, and Japan.

To get to the Indies, Europeans had to travel long land or sea routes. Columbus thought he could find an easier and faster sea route. He wasn't sure of this, but he was brave enough to try. He headed across the Atlantic Ocean with three ships: the *Niña*, the *Pinta*, and the *Santa María*. The ships had Spanish names because they were paid for by the king and queen of Spain.

After two months, Columbus reached land. He thought the land was India, so he called the people there Indians. But it wasn't India. It was an island in the Bahamas, which Columbus named San Salvador. He found more islands nearby. No Europeans at the time, including Columbus, knew of these places. That is why they called them a "new world."

Some people think that Christopher Columbus discovered America, but he didn't. The Arawak people had been living on San Salvador for a long time, and other native people lived in other places Columbus "found." Also, other explorers had sailed to America before Columbus. Still, it was Columbus's voyages that made America known to the European world.

Every year we observe Columbus Day in October because Columbus and his men reached America on October 12, 1492. Many people take pride in Christopher Columbus. The Italians are proud of him because he was born in Italy. The Spanish are proud of him because their country gave him the ships for his historic voyage.

Native Americans, or "Indians" as Columbus called them, feel differently. For them, Columbus is no hero because he began the European conquest of their homelands and their many peoples.

Marie Curie (1867–1934)
Pierre Curie (1859–1906)

They discovered radium.

Manya Sklodowska (Sklaw-DOV-ska) grew up in Warsaw, Poland. Her parents were teachers. When Manya was young, her father lost his job and her mother died. Despite many family hardships, both Manya and her sister, Bronya, wanted a good education. When they grew up, Bronya moved to Paris to become a doctor. Manya worked in Poland as a teacher to pay for her sister's education. Later, Manya moved to Paris to study math and science. In Paris, she met Pierre Curie (Cure-EE), a brilliant French scientist. They married in 1895, and Manya changed her name to Marie Curie.

Marie and Pierre worked together in a scientific laboratory. They experimented with strange metals that were radioactive. Radioactive materials send out a special kind of energy. The Curies discovered a new radioactive material, which they named "radium." They received many honors for their work, including the Nobel Prize in physics. The Nobel Prize is awarded each year to people who have made the world better.

In 1906, Pierre was killed as he walked in front of a horse-drawn wagon. Marie Curie was very unhappy, but with time she returned to her work. She took Pierre's teaching job at a French university called the Sorbonne (Sore-BUN) and ran their scientific laboratory herself. She earned a Nobel Prize in chemistry in 1911, becoming the first person ever to win two Nobel Prizes.

In 1934, Marie Curie died. The radioactive materials she used in her experiments were harmful to her health.

Today, scientists working with these same elements wear protective clothing and are very careful. When handled correctly, radium can be helpful to people. Doctors once used it to help cure cancer in people. Now they use safer radioactive materials.

Walt Disney (1901–1966)

He created Mickey Mouse and Disneyland.

Walt Disney was born in Chicago, but his family moved to a farm in Missouri when he was young. As a child, he enjoyed drawing. When he was 16, Walt went back to Chicago to study art. At the age of 19, he started making cartoon ads to be shown in movie theaters. He didn't earn much money, but he liked the work.

When he was 22, Walt Disney moved to Los Angeles, California. He was fascinated by cartoons. Cartoons are made by drawing many pictures and showing them one after another, so quickly that the pictures are animated, or seem to move.

Disney drew cartoons in his garage. He liked to make characters do funny things. When he was 27, he created Mickey Mouse. In the next ten years, Walt Disney invented Donald Duck, Goofy, Pluto, and other cartoon characters that are still famous today. Many people went to movie theaters to see his short cartoons. At last, Walt Disney was successful.

But Disney didn't want to make only short cartoons. He wanted to make a full-length animated film. He settled down to work and made the first long cartoon movie ever: *Snow White and the Seven Dwarfs*. He hired talented people to help him make the thousands of drawings needed for the movie. It was a hit. Walt Disney then made more long cartoons: *Pinocchio, Fantasia, Dumbo, Bambi, Cinderella, Alice in Wonderland, Peter Pan, Lady and the Tramp, 101 Dalmations*, and *The Jungle Book*.

So many movies! So much success! Yet Walt Disney had even more ideas. He created *Mary Poppins*, a movie with cartoons and people. His company today employs many people and continues to make imaginative movies like *Beauty and the Beast* and *The Little Mermaid*.

Walt Disney had another brainstorm. He wanted to make enormous amusement parks where people could enjoy themselves. When this idea came true, he named the parks after himself: Disneyland and Walt Disney World.

Amelia Earhart (1897–1937?)

She was a daring airplane pilot.

Amelia Earhart was born in Atchison, Kansas. When she grew up, she became a nurse. She nursed wounded soldiers in World War I and went on to study at Columbia University. But Amelia found that she didn't want to be a nurse or a university student. She wanted to become an airplane pilot.

Her dream surprised people. Airplanes had been invented around the time she was born. They were new and dangerous. Only the bravest men flew them, and people then did not expect women to try such risky adventures.

Nevertheless, in California, Amelia took a job to pay for flying lessons. She loved the excitement of flying. In 1928, she was the first female to fly as a passenger on a plane across the Atlantic Ocean. Afterwards, Amelia wrote a book that told about the trip. Her book was published by a man named George Putnam. Amelia and George fell in love and were married in 1931.

In 1932, Amelia Earhart flew across the Atlantic Ocean by herself. She was the first woman ever to do this. The trip took about 15 hours. Today, in a modern plane, the same trip would take about five hours. Amelia made other "first woman" trips, too. She flew solo from Hawaii to California and across the United States, first one way and then the other.

Amelia Earhart was a pilot who loved to challenge herself. Her next goal was to be the first woman to fly around the world.

In 1937, she and her co-pilot Fred Noonan began the trip. Unfortunately, they didn't make it. Amelia Earhart's plane was lost near New Guinea in the Pacific Ocean. No one has ever found any traces of Amelia or her plane, but people continue to search for them.

Why did she try such a daring flight? Amelia Earhart once explained her feelings by saying, "Adventure is worthwhile in itself."

Thomas Alva Edison (1847–1931)

He invented the electric light bulb, the record player, and many more amazing things.

Thomas Alva Edison was born in Milan, Ohio. The youngest of seven children, he was called Alva. Alva was a curious child, always asking his mother why things worked the way they did. He liked to experiment, too. Once he sat on some goose eggs to see if he could hatch them.

When Alva was seven, his family moved to Michigan. At school, he was whipped by the teacher for asking too many questions. When his mother found this out, she took Alva out of school. From then on, she taught him at home. She had been a teacher and tried to make learning fun for Alva.

As Thomas Alva Edison grew up, he began to invent things. At the age of 23, he figured out a better way to make a telegraph machine. He sold his plan for $40,000. With the money, he opened a workshop, or laboratory, in West Orange, New Jersey. There, he invented a better typewriter. He then moved to Menlo Park, New Jersey, and invented an improved telephone. Thomas Edison invented the record player (called a phonograph) in 1877. Two years later, he invented the electric light bulb. People called him the "Wizard of Menlo Park."

Edison's ears had been injured when he was a young man. As a result, his hearing was poor. As he grew older, his hearing grew worse, but Edison said his deafness helped him concentrate. He was happiest when he was inventing things in his laboratory.

Scientists work in different ways. George Washington Carver mostly worked alone. Marie and Pierre Curie worked together. Thomas Edison liked to work with a team of people. He said that genius was "1 percent inspiration and 99 percent perspiration." With a team of people, the perspiration part of the work could be shared and thus go faster. Edison received many awards for his work.

Albert Einstein (1879–1955)

He changed our ideas about time and space.

Albert Einstein was born in Germany, but when he grew up, he moved to Switzerland. He said it was a more peaceful country. Albert wanted peace so he could think about math and science.

When Albert was 26, he developed the "theory of relativity" to explain energy. The mathematical theory is complicated. Einstein said that probably only twelve people in the world would be able to understand it.

In 1905, Einstein became a physics professor at the University of Zurich in Switzerland. He later returned to Germany to teach and develop more ideas about energy, light, and time. In 1921, he won the Nobel Prize in physics. In addition to being a brilliant scientist, Einstein was an excellent violinist.

In 1933, Aldolf Hitler and the Nazis ruled Germany. They took Albert Einstein's job and home away from him because he was Jewish. The Nazis hated Jews. Fortunately, when his home was seized, Einstein was on a trip to England and the United States. He did not go back to Germany. Instead, he chose to live in the United States. From then on, Einstein worked and studied at the Institute for Advanced Study in Princeton, New Jersey.

In 1939, Einstein warned United States President Franklin D. Roosevelt that Hitler's scientists might try to make a powerful new atomic bomb in order to win World War II. Roosevelt asked American scientists to invent the bomb first. By the time the American bomb was ready, Germany had surrendered, or given up. However, the United States, England, and other allied countries were still fighting Japan.

The United States dropped two atomic bombs on Japan. The bombs killed many people, and Japan surrendered. The bomb helped America and the Allies win World War II, but Einstein was horrified by the bomb's power to kill. He became a tireless worker for peace and hoped that people's fear of atomic bombs would prevent future wars.

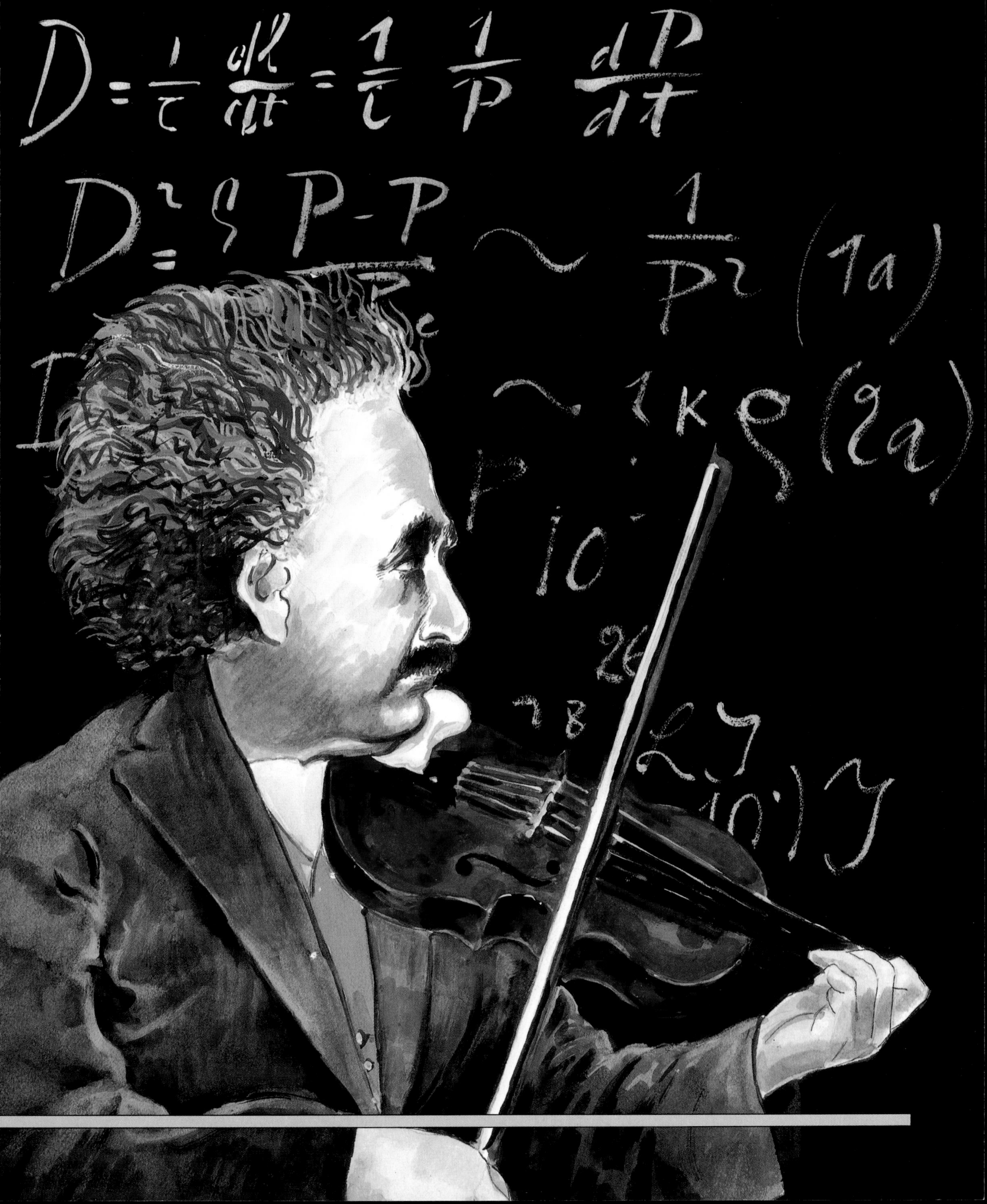

Elizabeth I (1533–1603)

She was queen in England's Golden Age.

Princess Elizabeth had red hair, as did her powerful father, King Henry VIII (the Eighth). At that time, the king was the most important man in all of England. Elizabeth's mother, Anne Boleyn, had been killed for disobeying him.

When King Henry VIII died, his son Edward became king. When Edward died, Henry's oldest daughter Mary Tudor became queen. When she died, it was Elizabeth's turn. In 1558, at the age of 25, Elizabeth became queen of England. Because she was the first queen named Elizabeth, she was called Elizabeth I (the First). At the time, the English felt that everyone in England should have the same religion, but they had fought over whether it should be Roman Catholic or Protestant. Elizabeth had been raised Protestant. To solve the religious problem, she reestablished the Church of England, which was similar to the Catholic church but was Protestant.

Elizabeth had another major problem. Her country had two enemies, France and Spain. Queen Elizabeth did not want England to go to war with either of them so she hinted that she would marry the French or Spanish king. Her hints helped to prevent war for many years, but she never married anyone.

Elizabeth had an enemy, a cousin who was called Mary Queen of Scots. Mary wanted to be queen of England and caused so much trouble that Elizabeth had her killed. A year later, in 1588, the king of Spain attacked England with a fleet of ships called the Spanish Armada. England defeated the Armada and became a strong world power.

Elizabeth was queen for 45 years—an era called the Golden Age of England. English explorers sailed around the world. Musicians and writers, including Shakespeare, wrote wonderful works. The queen of England today is Elizabeth II (the Second). Though still powerful, the British king or queen no longer rules the country. England is now led by an elected leader called the prime minister.

Duke Ellington (1899–1974)

He played and wrote music called jazz.

A pianist plays the piano. A composer writes music. A bandleader leads a band, and an orchestra leader leads an orchestra. Duke Ellington did all of these things. He was a brilliant musician, and his favorite music was jazz. Jazz is a type of music that was created mostly by African Americans.

Jazz grew in the early 1900's out of African rhythms, folk music, blues, gospel music, slave songs, and work songs. It continues to grow and change. Jazz musicians improvise, or make up, parts of the music while they play. When they play together, they usually take turns improvising. Some jazz pieces are slow, and some are fast. Many different kinds of instruments are used to play jazz, and jazz songs are sung by jazz singers.

Edward Kennedy Ellington was born in Washington, D.C. He was nicknamed "Duke" by his family. Duke took piano lessons when he was young. But it wasn't until he was a teenager that he decided to take his lessons seriously.

Duke practiced hard and became a jazz pianist. When he grew older, he became a bandleader. The musicians he chose for his band were the very best. People listened to them on radios and record players.

The more popular Duke Ellington became, the bigger his band grew until it was big enough sometimes to be called an orchestra.

The Duke Ellington Band played at The Cotton Club in Harlem. Harlem is the section of New York City where Duke Ellington lived. The band also traveled to other cities in the United States and to Europe.

Duke Ellington wrote songs, often with his friend Billy Strayhorn. They wrote "Mood Indigo" and "Sophisticated Lady." They wrote "Take the A Train" about a subway train in New York City that still goes through Harlem. Duke Ellington also wrote movie music, religious music, and music that celebrated African American people.

We the People

Benjamin Franklin (1706–1790)

He was a writer, printer, scientist, inventor, and leader.

Born in Boston, Massachusetts, Benjamin Franklin was the fifteenth child in a family of 17 children. He went to school for only two years, but he read enough books at home to educate himself. When he was 12, Ben went to work in his brother's print shop. At 17, he moved to Philadelphia, Pennsylvania, where he found another job as a printer.

In time, Ben Franklin owned his own print shop in Philadelphia and became a publisher. A publisher is someone who prints and sells books, magazines, and newspapers. Franklin published a newspaper and a yearly book called *Poor Richard's Almanac*. In the *Almanac* he gave advice, such as "God helps them that help themselves," and "Early to bed, Early to rise, Makes a man healthy, wealthy, and wise."

Franklin helped Philadelphia by starting a library, a fire department, and a school that became the University of Pennsylvania. Though he owned a few slaves, he became an abolitionist and wanted to abolish slavery. He helped Thomas Jefferson write the Declaration of Independence, which explained why Americans felt they had to fight the English for independence. Franklin helped America win the Revolutionary War by getting the French to fight against the English, too.

Benjamin Franklin also liked to experiment. Once, he flew a kite during a thunderstorm to see what would happen. A flash of lightning struck the kite and went down the wet string to the key at the end. Anyone who touched the key felt an electrical shock. From this experiment (which is dangerous—don't try it!), Franklin invented the lightning rod. He also invented bifocal glasses and the Franklin stove.

In 1787, at the age of 81, Benjamin Franklin helped others write the Constitution of the United States. The Constitution begins with the famous words, "We the people . . ." and describes the U.S. government and its basic laws.

Mohandas Gandhi (1869–1948)

He taught the world how to win power without fighting.

Mohandas Gandhi was born in 1869 in Porbandar, India. When he became a great leader, people called him Mahatma, which means "Great Soul." As a young man, Gandhi went to England to become a lawyer. Gandhi went back to India and then traveled to South Africa. There, he helped Indians like himself be treated more fairly by white rulers.

Twenty-one years later, he returned to India to help the Indians there. The rulers in both South Africa and India were English. The English were rich, and the Indians were poor. Gandhi helped the Indians become powerful in several ways. First he taught the Indians to spin and weave their own cotton cloth. He and his followers wore simple clothes made from this cloth. By buying from themselves instead of from the English, the Indians gained financial power.

The English also had guns. Gandhi suggested the Indian people fight back without guns and violence. He told them to disobey unfair laws. He also advised them to go peacefully when arrested and taken to jail. Gandhi said it was honorable to be arrested for a good cause. He went to jail many times.

Sometimes Gandhi fasted, or didn't eat, for days in order to call attention to an injustice. Gandhi also told people to go on strike, or not work for unfair bosses. He told them to boycott, or refuse to buy things, from unfair store owners. "If people hit you," he said, "don't hit back."

Gandhi's plans for non-violence worked. As the harshness of the English was seen by more and more people, the Indians grew more powerful. Slowly, they won their freedom from England. But their troubles were not over. Indians fought for power against other Indians. At the age of 78, Gandhi was shot and killed.

Today Gandhi is called the Father of India. His brave way of fighting inspired people around the world. Cesar Chavez, Rosa Parks, and Martin Luther King, Jr., all learned from Mahatma Gandhi.

Katsushika Hokusai (1760–1849)

He loved to draw and lived to draw.

Katsushika Hokusai was born near Tokyo, Japan. From an early age, he loved to draw, and this love stayed with him all his life. Hokusai lived until he was 89. During his lifetime he made 40,000 drawings and over 10,000 woodcuts. A woodcut is a print made by pressing a piece of paper onto a carved and inked block of wood.

Hokusai was born poor and stayed poor for most of his life. But he was rich in artistic spirit. He was always excited about the next drawing he was going to do and the next woodcut he was going to make. He liked to change what he drew and how he drew. Each time he changed his drawing style, he changed his name. He changed his name more than thirty times, but the name he used most was Hokusai.

Hokusai's most famous pictures are of people, animals, ocean waves, and a mountain in Japan called Mt. Fuji. He also published drawing books that showed how to draw animals and people. The text is written in Japanese. Japanese is written in vertical, or up-and-down, columns, instead of in horizontal rows like the words in this book.

At the age of 75, Hokusai wrote this about his life's work: "Since the age of six, I have had a passion for drawing things. Now that I am 75, I have finally learned something of the true quality of birds, animals, insects, fishes, and of the vital nature of grasses and trees. By the time I am 89, I shall have made more progress. By the time I am 90, I shall understand the deeper meaning of things. When I am 100, I shall be truly marvelous; and at 110 each dot and each line will possess a life of its own."

Hokusai was an artist who always wanted to do better and loved the challenge of trying to do so.

Thomas Jefferson (1743–1826)

He wrote the Declaration of Independence.

Born in Virginia, Thomas Jefferson was the son of a well-to-do plantation owner. When his father died, Thomas was only 14. As the oldest boy, he became the owner of the plantation, which his guardian took care of for him. At the age of 16, Thomas Jefferson went to college. Then, like Gandhi and Lincoln, he became a lawyer.

In 1776, America was getting ready to fight the Revolutionary War to gain freedom from England. At the time, Americans were ruled by England (also called Great Britain). Americans needed a statement to explain to England why they now wanted to run their own country. Benjamin Franklin and others contributed ideas for the declaration, but the strong and beautiful words were Thomas Jefferson's. "We hold these truths to be self-evident," he wrote. "That all men are created equal; that they are endowed by their Creator with certain unalienable rights; that among these are life, liberty, and the pursuit of happiness."

America won the Revolutionary War and became the United States of America. George Washington was elected to be the first president, John Adams was the second, and Thomas Jefferson was the third.

But Thomas Jefferson was more than a leader and lawmaker. He designed his Virginia home, called Monticello (Mon-te-CHEL-lo). He invented a lap desk and a plow. He played violin while his wife, Martha, played the harpsichord. He also grew beautiful flowers, herbs, and vegetables in huge gardens at Monticello. Jefferson owned many slaves, yet he thought slavery was cruel. He wanted to write something against the practice of slavery in the Declaration of Independence but was out-voted.

As an educator, Thomas Jefferson founded the University of Virginia. He also designed some of its loveliest buildings. Jefferson's picture is on the nickel. When you turn the nickel over, you will see Monticello.

Helen Keller (1880–1968)
Anne Sullivan (1866–1936)

A child who could neither see nor hear was taught by a patient teacher.

Helen Keller was born in Tuscumbia, Alabama. When she was two, she became sick. As a result, she lost her sense of sight and her sense of hearing. Because Helen couldn't hear, she couldn't speak. She lived in a dark world of her own until she was seven years old. Then, a 20-year-old teacher, Anne Sullivan, came to live with Helen and her family.

Anne Sullivan also had been blind as a child. But she had been operated on and could see better, though not perfectly. Anne taught Helen by spelling words on her hand. Once she understood what Anne was doing, Helen learned quickly. She learned to read and write Braille, a system of writing for the blind that uses raised dots. She also learned to "read" faces. She could understand what people said by touching their faces as they spoke. She learned to write on a special typewriter. By the time she was 16, Helen had learned to speak, though she was hard to understand.

Helen Keller was tutored in high school classes and went to Radcliffe College, then the women's college at Harvard University. Anne Sullivan went with her. In 1904, Helen Keller graduated with honors.

For the rest of her life, Helen Keller helped others with physical disabilities. She traveled to other countries and gave speeches. She also wrote books and received many honors. In *The Story of My Life*, Helen Keller wrote about her love for books. She said, "No barrier of the senses shuts me out from . . . my book-friends. They talk to me without embarrassment or awkwardness."

Helen Keller believed people should help one another. She said we would get along better if we imagined ourselves belonging to one worldwide family.

Martin Luther King, Jr. (1929–1968)
Rosa Parks (1913–)

They challenged segregation and won.

Rosa Parks and Martin Luther King, Jr., grew up in states where the segregation, or separation, of black people and white people was a way of life. Unfair laws separated African Americans from whites in schools, in restaurants, and on buses.

When Rosa Parks grew up, she became a tailor's assistant in Montgomery, Alabama. She also worked for the local NAACP, the National Association for the Advancement of Colored People. The NAACP decided to challenge bus segregation, and Rosa Parks offered to help. In 1955, at the age of 43, she refused to give up her seat on a bus to a white man. She was arrested.

After her arrest, African Americans in Montgomery, led by the Reverend Martin Luther King, Jr., began a bus strike, or boycott. For one year, black people in Montgomery walked, rode bicycles, and drove cars to work. They refused to pay to ride an unfair bus, and the bus company lost money. Their peaceful protest worked, and the unfair law was changed.

Martin Luther King, Jr., was born in Atlanta, Georgia. He became a minister. Using the peaceful methods of Gandhi, King battled segregation in schools and elsewhere. He was joined by many other brave black people, including children, and by brave white people, too. Their struggle to get the government to enforce the rights of black people is called the Civil Rights Movement. One of the many songs they sang to keep their hopes up in hard times was "We Shall Overcome."

When Martin Luther King, Jr., spoke, people listened. In 1963, he gave a speech to half a million people in which he said, "I have a dream that my four little children will one day live in a nation where they will not be judged by the color of their skin but by the content of their character." In 1964, he received the Nobel Peace Prize. When Martin Luther King, Jr., was 39, he was shot and killed. He is honored on his birthday every January with a national holiday.

Leonardo da Vinci (1452–1519)

He was both a painter and an inventor.

Leonardo da Vinci (VIN-chee) painted two of the most famous paintings in the world. The *Mona Lisa* is a portrait of a woman with a mysterious smile. Viewers debate if she actually is smiling, and they wonder what she is thinking.

Leonardo da Vinci also painted *The Last Supper*, a picture of Jesus and his 12 disciples. Leonardo painted it on a wall in a church in Milan, Italy. The painting has flaked and faded over 500 years. It is now being restored, or fixed, so that people can still enjoy it.

In addition to being a painter, Leonardo was a scientist and an inventor. He studied plants, animals, and the human body. He drew pictures that show how birds fly, how muscles are attached to bones, and what different plants and trees look like. Sometimes he wrote secret notes on his drawings in backwards writing. To read the notes, you have to look at them in a mirror.

Leonardo da Vinci invented weapons, an alarm clock that worked by water, a parachute, and a flying machine. He made a model of the flying machine with wood, cloth, and feathers. This machine had wings that flapped like a bird's. It is said that one of his students tried the machine and broke his leg when it crashed.

Leonardo da Vinci lived at a time now called the Italian Renaissance (REN-uh-sanz). The Renaissance took place between 1300 and 1500. Wealthy people and church leaders in Italy hired artists to make statues and paint pictures for them. Some of Italy's greatest painters of all time, such as Botticelli (Bot-uh-CHEL-lee), Michelangelo (My-kell-AN-jel-lo), Raphael (Raff-ay-YELL), and Leonardo all painted during the great Italian Renaissance.

49

Abraham Lincoln (1809–1865)

He became president and helped to free the slaves.

Abraham Lincoln was born in a log cabin in Kentucky on February 12, 1809. When he was seven, Abe's family moved to the Indiana frontier, where new settlers were moving. Only a few schools had been built, so young Abe read books at home, often by firelight. He wrote with charcoal on a shovel or board because he had no pencils and paper.

When he was 22, Abraham Lincoln moved to New Salem, Illinois. People liked to hear him speak. They elected him to the Illinois legislature, the group of leaders who make laws for the state. Abe taught himself to be a lawyer. He ran against Stephen A. Douglas for election to the United States Senate, a group that makes laws for the country.

Lincoln lost, but in the process he became known for his speeches against slavery. In Southern states, white farm owners owned black slaves. In the North, white factory owners did not own their workers, but they paid them very low wages. Most Northerners were against slavery; most Southerners were for it because they felt they needed it. In 1860, Northerners helped elect Lincoln president of the United States.

A Civil War broke out between the North and the South. The South wanted to become a separate country. President Lincoln and the North wanted the United States to remain whole. During the war, President Lincoln issued the Emancipation Proclamation, which led to the end of slavery. In the same year, 1863, he gave a speech after the Battle of Gettysburg. In his address, he referred back to 1776, the year the United States was born. Lincoln now asked for "a new birth of freedom" so that the "government of the people, by the people, for the people, shall not perish from the earth." Under Lincoln's leadership, the United States remained one country.

Abraham Lincoln was shot and killed at the age of 56. His picture is on the penny and the five dollar bill. Turn them over to see his beautiful memorial in Washington, D.C. We celebrate Lincoln's birthday along with George Washington's on Presidents Day in February.

Four score and seven years ago our fathers brought
forth, upon this continent, a new nation, conceived
in liberty, and dedicated to the proposition that
all men are created equal.
Now we are engaged in a great civil war, testing
whether that nation, or any nation so conceived,
and so dedicated, can long endure. We are met
on a great battle field of that war. We have
come to dedicate a portion of that field, as a final
resting place for those who here gave their lives
that the nation might live.

Yo-Yo Ma (1955–)

He's one of the best cellists in the world.

A cellist (CHEL-list) is someone who plays the cello (CHEL-low). A cello is like a big violin. It is too big to be held under your chin so it rests on the floor. A cello makes a lower sound than a violin.

Yo-Yo Ma is one of the finest cellists in the world. He was born in Paris, France, to Chinese parents. Both his mother and his father are musical and well-educated. Yo-Yo and his sister were taught music and school subjects at an early age. At age five, he played both the cello and the piano at a concert at the University of Paris.

When Yo-Yo was seven, his family moved to New York City. He continued to play the cello and surprised his teachers by memorizing his lessons. When he was a teenager, Yo-Yo felt rebellious and didn't want to practice. But he didn't give up because he knew the cello was important to him.

Many musicians study only music. Yo-Yo Ma decided to go to Harvard University to study music and other subjects, as well. His sister made a similar choice. She continued to study piano and also became a pediatrician.

Sometimes Yo-Yo Ma would leave Harvard to give concerts. He performed with some of the best-known orchestras in the world. During the summer, he performed at the Marlboro Music Festival in Vermont. There he met Jill Horner, who was helping to run the festival. They fell in love, were married, and now have two children.

Yo-Yo Ma continues to perform brilliantly around the world. Sometimes he plays alone; sometimes he plays with others. Certain old cellos made by great craftsmen sound better than newer cellos. Yo-Yo Ma has two cellos, each more than 250 years old. One of Yo-Yo Ma's favorite musicians is the German composer Johann Sebastian Bach (1685–1750). Bach wrote beautiful music for the cello.

Yo-Yo Ma's father told his son to play a little of Bach's music each night before bed. "This is not practicing," his father explained. "This is for you."

Gabriela Mistral (1889–1957)

She won the Nobel Prize for literature in 1945.

Gabriela Mistral was born in Vicuña, Chile, a country in South America. As a child, Gabriela's name was Lucila Godoy Alcayaga. Young Lucila loved to read, write, and sing. At the age of fifteen, she became a teacher. Each day she walked or rode a horse through the beautiful Chilean countryside to a small, rural schoolhouse. She was an excellent teacher who made education delightful for her students. She liked to take her children outside *en un corro bajo el sol* (together under the sun) to enjoy and study nature.

But teaching was not her only skill. Lucila also wrote poetry about nature and poor people. She wanted to send her poems to newspapers and magazines, but she was afraid that school officials would not like them.

One day Lucila thought of a solution to this problem. She created a new name for her poet self. When writers change their names this way, their writing names are called pen names. For the first part of her pen name, Lucila chose Gabriela after the angel Gabriel, the bearer of good news in the Bible. For the last part, she chose *mistral*, the Spanish word for wind.

Lucila entered her poems in a poetry contest for all the writers in Chile. She won as Gabriela Mistral.

Gabriela Mistral became famous both for her teaching and her writing. She helped to improve schools in Chile and Mexico, and was honored for these achievements. But the most important honor she ever received was for her poetry.

In 1945, Gabriela Mistral was awarded the Nobel Prize for literature. She was the first Latin American writer ever to win this splendid award. (Latin Americans live in countries south of the United States. They are called Latin Americans because they speak Spanish or Portuguese, languages that developed from an older language called Latin.)

The Magic Flute

Don Giovanni

The Marriage of Figaro

Così Fan Tutte

56

Wolfgang Amadeus Mozart (1756–1791)

He was a musical genius who began to write music when he was five.

Wolfgang Amadeus Mozart (MOTE-zart) was born in Salzburg, Austria, where his father wrote music for the emperor. Wolfgang was very musical as a child. At age 3, he began to play the harpsichord, which is like a piano. At 4, Wolfgang learned how to play the violin. At 5, he wrote music. At 6, Mozart's father took Wolfgang to Austria to play for the emperor and empress. They were amazed to see a young child play so well. At 7, Wolfgang played for people in Paris, France, and London, England.

Wolfgang never went to school. His father was his teacher. By age 13, Wolfgang was writing music for the archbishop of Salzburg. Later, he moved to Vienna, the capital of Austria. There, he performed, gave lessons, and composed music. He worked hard, but he was not always successful. Even though Mozart was a musical genius, he was poor. He could not make enough money to support his family. Mozart died at age 36. When he died, he had written over 600 musical compositions. His music is greatly loved today.

Wolfgang Amadeus Mozart wrote 22 operas. An opera is a special musical show with a story acted out by singers. His operas, such as *The Magic Flute, Don Giovanni, Cosi Fan Tutte,* and *The Marriage of Figaro,* are often performed today. Some have been made into movies. Mozart composed 41 symphonies, including the *Jupiter Symphony.* A symphony is music for many instruments to play together. He also wrote church music and musical pieces called sonatas.

You can hear Mozart's delightful music on classical radio stations, on tapes and CD's, on TV, and in musical theaters. Every year in Salzburg, the town where Mozart was born, there is a special music festival that features his music. Many other cities have Mozart festivals, too.

Jesse Owens (1913–1980)

He was one of the greatest athletes who ever lived.

Jesse Owens was born in Oakville, Alabama, in 1913. He was the son of a sharecropper. A sharecropper is someone who farms someone else's land in return for a small amount of crops and usually poor housing. When Jesse was 7, his family moved to Cleveland, Ohio.

When he was in junior high school, Jesse tried out for the track team. Coach Charles Riley was amazed when Jesse ran the 100-yard dash in ten seconds. Coach Riley helped Jesse become a high school track star. At Ohio State University, Jesse broke world records in long jumping, hurdle racing, and flat racing. In the long jump, athletes see how far they can jump with one leap. In a hurdle race, runners run and jump over fences on the track. In a flat race, runners run as fast as they can on a flat track.

After college, Jesse was ready for the Olympic Games. The Olympics are held every four years in a different country. Athletes from around the world compete.

In 1936, the Olympics were held in Berlin, Germany. The leader of Germany then was Adolf Hitler. He and his Nazi followers believed that white German people were better than black people and Jewish people. They were enraged as they watched Jesse Owens, an African American, win four gold medals.

But not all Germans felt the same way as Hitler. In one event, Jesse Owens was helped by a German athlete, Lutz Long. Lutz watched Jesse run mistakenly and step on the takeoff board twice before his long jump. This was not allowed. If Jesse stepped on the board a third time, he would be out of the contest. Lutz told Jesse to place a towel six inches in front of the takeoff to avoid another foul. It worked.

Jesse Owens set seven world records in his lifetime. When he stopped racing, he gave speeches about sports. He said that athletes should be honest and live good, healthy lives.

Peter the Great (1672–1725)

He modernized the country of Russia.

Long ago the ruler or king of Russia was called the czar (ZAR). Peter the Great became czar of Russia when he was 17 years old. When he was growing up near Moscow, Peter met people from European countries west of Russia, countries such as England and Holland. As czar, he kept in touch with people from these countries. Peter felt that Russian people could learn much about western soldiers, ships, and factories.

Historians often say that Peter "westernized" Russia. By that, they mean that he brought European ideas for clothes, schools, the government, the calendar, and the alphabet into Russia. He also built a new, European-type city, which he named St. Petersburg.

Peter the Great worked hard for his country. He made the Russian army stronger, and he built the Russian navy. He conquered land on the Baltic Sea to give Russia a place for its ships.

Historians have mixed feelings about Peter the Great. Some think it is good that he made Russia a more modern, up-to-date country. Others think Peter should not have westernized Russia. They point out that he was a very cruel ruler. He forced serfs, who were like slaves, to work in factories; and he tried to rule the Russian church.

Other Russian czars were also cruel to their people. In 1917, people rebelled against a czar called Nicholas II (the Second). The rebels were led by a man named V.I. Lenin. Lenin set up a new kind of government that had no czar. The new system was called communism. Under communist rule, St. Petersburg's name was changed to Leningrad. In 1991, the Russian people rebelled against communist rule because it was not working. They are now setting up a new government that they hope will work better. One of the first things the Russian people did was to change the name of Leningrad back to its old name, St. Petersburg.

Beatrix Potter (1866–1943)

She wrote and illustrated *The Tale of Peter Rabbit.*

Beatrix Potter was born in London, England, to a well-to-do family. As a child, she spent most of her time in a room called the nursery. Her nurse was not a doctor's nurse, but a child-care worker trained to raise children at home. When Beatrix was six, her brother Bertram was born. The nurse took care of him, too. Beatrix's favorite activities were reading, drawing, and painting.

Beatrix's father often took his family to the country, where Beatrix drew birds, rabbits, and flowers. She never went to school. A teacher called a governess and a drawing teacher taught her in her room. For company Beatrix had her teachers, her brother, and many pets. In the nursery she drew pictures of her frogs, lizards, mice, and turtles.

When Bertram went away to boarding school, the governess left. Beatrix Potter was then 17. Her mother hired a new teacher named Annie Carter to come to the house. Only three years older than Beatrix, Annie became Beatrix's first friend. When Annie married, she stopped teaching Beatrix, but the two young women remained good friends. Beatrix grew to love Annie's children.

One day, to amuse Annie's son Noel, Beatrix Potter wrote him a letter. In it she said, "My dear Noel, I don't know what to write to you, so I shall tell you a story about four little rabbits whose names were Flopsy, Mopsy, Cottontail, and Peter." In 1901, this story was published as *The Tale of Peter Rabbit*. It became very popular. Beatrix Potter wrote and illustrated many more books, such as *The Tale of Benjamin Bunny* and *The Tale of Jemima Puddle-Duck*. In these stories, animals dress and act like people. When she was 47, Beatrix Potter moved to northern England and became a successful sheep farmer.

Eleanor Roosevelt (1884–1962)
Franklin Roosevelt (1882–1945)

They were both great leaders.

Eleanor Roosevelt was born in New York City to a wealthy family. Franklin Delano Roosevelt was born in Hyde Park, New York, also to a wealthy family. They were distant cousins. When they grew up, they married and had five children.

Franklin became a lawyer and then a lawmaker in New York State. In 1920, he ran for vice-president of the United States but lost. The next year, Franklin got polio and could no longer walk. (Today children are given medicine so they won't get this disease.) Franklin used leg braces, a wheelchair, and crutches. With Eleanor's help, he went back to work and, in 1928, was elected governor of New York State.

Franklin D. Roosevelt (nicknamed FDR) was elected president of the United States in 1932, the time of the Great Depression. American businesses were not doing well, and many people were poor. Roosevelt promised them a "new deal." He said, "The only thing we have to fear is fear itself." He started the social security program so that people would receive money when they grew old and could no longer work. He also started programs to help farmers, artists, the sick, and the jobless.

During World War II, England was bombed by Hitler's Nazis. Winston Churchill asked for help. The United States did help, as did Russia and other countries. As a result, the United States, England, and their allies won the war.

Eleanor Roosevelt helped her husband with his work. She also worked on her own to help young people and poor people. After Franklin died, she served as U.S. delegate to the United Nations. In 1948, she helped write the Universal Declaration of Human Rights, which says that all people around the world are born free and equal. The wife of the U.S. president is called the First Lady. People honored Eleanor Roosevelt by calling her First Lady of the World.

FDR's picture can be found on dimes.

Sequoya (*c.* 1760–1843)

He invented a written language for the Cherokee.

Sequoya (Sih-KWOY-yuh), a Cherokee, was born in Loudon County, Tennessee. His people and other native peoples had been living in America for thousands of years before Christopher Columbus and other European explorers arrived.

When Sequoya grew up, he became a silversmith. A silversmith is someone who designs and makes things like jewelry from silver. Sequoya traded his jewelry with other American Indians and with the new settlers. He couldn't read, but he was very interested in English newspapers. He understood that the ink marks on the pages were a way of recording their spoken words. The Cherokees had no way to do this.

Sequoya solved the problem by inventing a kind of alphabet called a syllabary for writing Cherokee. He taught the Cherokees to read it and wrote articles about Cherokee history for them to read. Cherokee newspapers were published using Sequoya's syllabary. The written language helped the Cherokee Nation, formed in 1827, become more powerful.

But it wasn't powerful enough. More and more Europeans came from overseas to the United States. Looking for places to live, they fought the Indians and pushed them off their homelands.

When gold was discovered in Cherokee territory, more white settlers came. Sequoya went to Washington, D.C., to ask the white lawmakers to protect Cherokee land. The United States government refused. Government leaders told the Cherokees they would have to leave. Most of the Cherokees were forced by U.S. soldiers in 1838–39 to walk 800 miles to Oklahoma. Thousands died on this long and difficult march called the "Trail of Tears."

Sequoya did not go on the march. It is said that he went to Mexico to continue his study of Indian languages. It was in Mexico that Sequoya died. The huge redwood trees in Sequoia National Park in California are named in his honor.

William Shakespeare (1564–1616)

He was the greatest English playwright who ever lived.

A playwright writes plays, an actor acts in them, and a poet writes poems. William Shakespeare did all three. He was born in Stratford-on-Avon in England. His family was neither rich nor poor; they were comfortably in-between. William went to school and probably read the works of ancient Greek and Roman writers. He probably also saw traveling theater companies perform in his town. When he was 18, he married Anne Hathaway. In the next three years, they had a daughter and a set of twins.

Sometime in the next seven years, William Shakespeare went to London to become an actor and a playwright. By the time he was 30, six of his plays had been performed in London. The queen at the time was Elizabeth I. When she died in 1603, her cousin James I became king. Like Elizabeth I, he enjoyed the theater and supported Shakespeare and other actors. Shakespeare usually wrote two plays a year. He went back and forth between London and his home in Stratford. At the age of 52, he died on his birthday, April 23.

William Shakespeare's plays are about all kinds of people. In *A Midsummer Night's Dream* a girl is put under a spell that makes her love a man with a donkey's head. In *Hamlet* a young prince looks at a skull and wonders about life and death. *Macbeth* begins with witches predicting disaster for a king. *King Lear* is about an old king who loses his throne.

People study Shakespeare's plays to better understand his language, which is five hundred years old and therefore a little different from the English people speak today. But though he wrote long ago, Shakespeare wrote in a creative and vivid way about feelings people still have. That is why people still like his plays and often quote lines from them, such as "Lord, what fools these mortals be!" and "All the world's a stage."

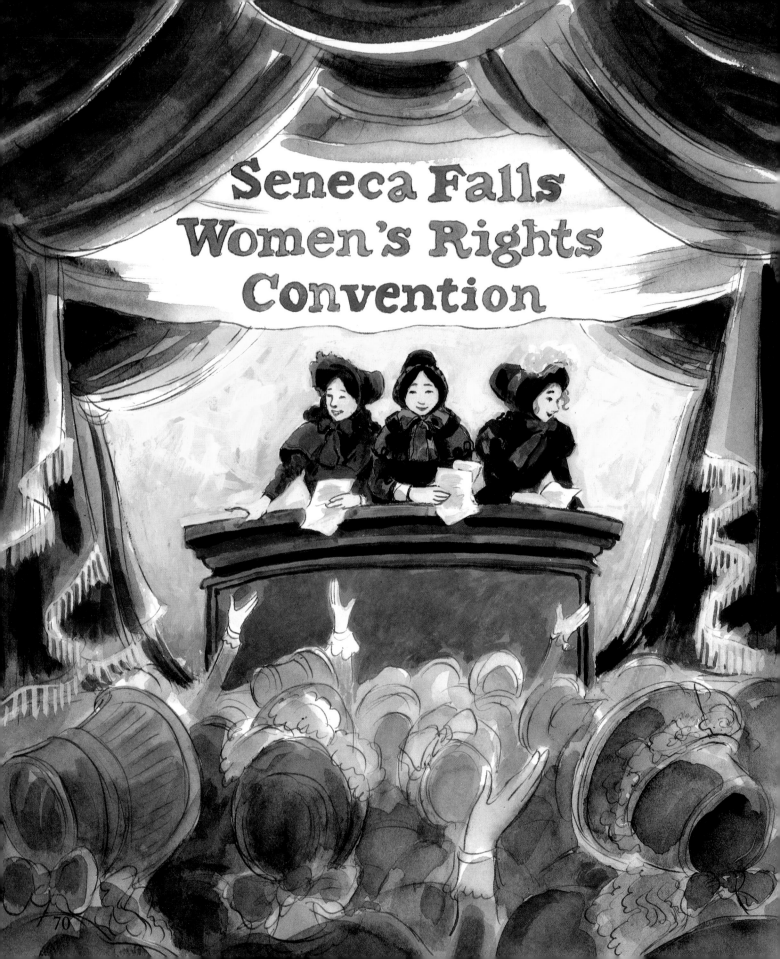

Elizabeth Cady Stanton (1815–1902)
Lucretia Mott (1793–1880)
Susan B. Anthony (1820–1906)

They wanted blacks to have the same rights as whites, and women to have the same rights as men.

Elizabeth Cady Stanton was born in Johnstown, New York. Lucretia Mott was born in Nantucket, Massachusetts, and Susan B. Anthony was born in Adams, Massachusetts. All three Northerners became abolitionists as adults. The abolitionists wanted to abolish, or end, slavery. They felt that white people had no right to own black people.

In 1840, Stanton and Mott went to an abolitionist meeting in England. At the meeting, the men wouldn't let the women sit with them. Mott and Stanton were angry. They felt that men had no right to treat women unfairly. In 1848, they held a meeting of their own in Seneca Falls, New York. It was the first women's rights convention ever held. At the convention, Stanton wrote a Declaration of Sentiments, which was like Thomas Jefferson's Declaration of Independence. But she added two important words. "We hold these truths to be self-evident: that all men *and women* are created equal; that they are endowed by their Creator with certain inalienable rights; that among these are life, liberty, and the pursuit of happiness."

In 1851, Stanton met Susan B. Anthony, and they became friends. In 1869, they started the National Woman Suffrage Association. Suffrage is the right to vote. At the time, women in the United States were not allowed to vote. Elizabeth Cady Stanton, Susan B. Anthony, and Lucretia Mott worked hard for women's suffrage. They wrote and spoke at meetings all over the country. Because of their work and the work of many who came after them, women finally were given the right to vote in 1920. Neither Stanton, Mott, or Anthony lived to see that happy day. But they did live long enough to see slavery abolished in 1865. They are honored with life-size statues at the Women's Rights National Historical Park in Seneca Falls, New York.

Maria Tallchief (1925–)
George Balanchine (1904–1983)

She was a ballerina; he was a choreographer.

Maria Tallchief was born Elizabeth Marie Tallchief in Fairfax, Oklahoma. When she was little, she was called Betty Marie. Tallchief is an American Indian name. Her mother was Scots-Irish; her father was Osage. Betty Marie began dance lessons when she was four years old. She also took piano lessons and excelled at both. When Betty Marie was 12, she gave a special concert. During the first half, she played the piano. During the second half, she danced.

Betty Marie practiced dance and piano through high school and then made up her mind which to pursue. After graduation, she went to New York City to become a ballerina. There she danced so well that she was hired by the *Ballet Russe de Monte Carlo*. She changed her name from Betty Marie to Maria.

A famous Russian choreographer named George Balanchine (BAL-an-cheen) had also joined the *Ballet Russe*. A choreographer designs a dance by putting dance steps to the music. George Balanchine worked with Maria and helped her to become a star. For several years, he and Maria were married.

George Balanchine's ballets were new and different. Some of them tell stories; others express the music and do not tell stories. In 1948, Balanchine became artistic director and main choreographer for the New York City Ballet. He created a version of Igor Stravinsky's *Firebird* especially for Maria. In this ballet, Maria danced the part of a magical wild bird.

Maria Tallchief also danced the part of Odette, queen of the swans in *Swan Lake*, and the part of the Sugar Plum Fairy in *The Nutcracker*, both composed by Peter Tchaikovsky (Cha-KOFF-skee). When she was 35, she became prima, or first, ballerina for the American Ballet Theatre.

At the age of 41, Maria Tallchief hung up her shoes. That is the ballet world's way of saying that she retired.

Harriet Tubman (c. 1820–1913)
Frederick Douglass (c. 1818–1895)

They escaped from slavery and then helped other slaves become free.

Harriet Tubman and Frederick Douglass were born as slaves in different parts of Maryland. When they grew up, they each ran away from their owners because they wanted to escape the brutal life of slavery. Slaves were controlled by their masters. They were beaten if their masters didn't like their work. They also could be sold to other owners and be taken away from their families.

Kind white and black people in the North helped runaway slaves by showing them where to go and letting them hide in their homes. These people ran what they called the Underground Railroad, which wasn't a railroad at all. It was a way of helping slaves escape from the South, where slavery was a way of life, to the North, where it usually wasn't. When Harriet Tubman reached the North, she acted with great courage. Instead of staying where she could be free, she sneaked back south 19 times to help other slaves escape, too.

Frederick Douglass was born Frederick Baily. He changed his name when he reached the North, so his Southern owner couldn't find him and take him back. He practiced reading and writing skills he had managed to learn as a slave, even though the education of slaves was illegal. In the North, Douglass was invited to an abolitionist meeting and asked to speak about freedom. He spoke so well that he soon became a famous anti-slavery speaker. He wrote an autobiography, or book about his life, and published a newspaper called the *North Star*. He also hid runaway slaves in his home in Rochester, New York.

During the Civil War, both Tubman and Douglass worked to help the North. In 1865, the Thirteenth Amendment to the U.S. Constitution officially ended slavery. In 1870, African American men were given the right to vote. Both Tubman and Douglass thought women should be able to vote, too, but that right wasn't given to women until 1920.

George Washington (1732–1799)

He was the first president of the United States.

George Washington was born on February 22, 1732, in Westmoreland County, Virginia. His family owned plantations worked by African American slaves. At the end of his life, George Washington freed his slaves.

When young George grew up, he became a farmer and then a land surveyor, whose job was to measure land. Later, he became a soldier in a Virginia regiment. At the time, America was a colony belonging to a faraway country named England. Many Americans didn't want to be part of England anymore. They felt that England was treating them unfairly.

George Washington, Benjamin Franklin, Thomas Jefferson, and other Americans wanted to form and rule their own nation. In 1776, Thomas Jefferson wrote the Declaration of Independence to tell England why America wanted to be free. But England did not want to give America freedom, so England and America went to war. This war was called the Revolutionary War or the War for Independence. George Washington was the general in charge of the American army. He was a strong, smart leader, and America won the war.

A new country was born, called the United States of America. Many people wanted George Washington to be king of the new country. But he felt it was wrong for America to have a king. In 1789, George Washington was elected to be the first president. At the time, the American flag had 13 stars arranged in a circle. Each star stood for a state. As the United States grew, more states and stars were added.

Every February, we celebrate George Washington's birthday and Abraham Lincoln's birthday on Presidents Day. Washington, D.C., is the capital of the United States. Named for George Washington, it is where the government of the United States meets and where the president lives. In Washington, D.C., you can climb the tall, pointed Washington Monument and look out over the whole city. George Washington's picture can be found on quarters and one dollar bills.

Babe Didrikson Zaharias (1914–1956)

She was the greatest female athlete of her time.

Mildred Ella Didrikson was born in Port Arthur, Texas. Her parents were from Norway. As a child, she played baseball so well that kids called her "Babe," after Babe Ruth. Babe Ruth was a famous slugger who played for the New York Yankees.

Babe played basketball in high school and then for a semi-pro team called the Golden Cyclones. (Semi-pro players are allowed to earn money; school players are not.) The Cyclones won the national championship. In both 1930 and 1931, Babe was named to the all-American women's basketball team by the Amateur Athletic Union.

Babe also was a track star. In 1932, she went to the Olympic Games and won gold medals for the women's 80-meter hurdles and the javelin throw. A javelin is like a long spear. Athletes compete to see who can throw it the greatest distance.

Babe also played tennis, and she was a diver and bowler, too. Now she wondered, *What other sports should I try?* A friend suggested golf. Babe learned the sport and soon began to win tournaments. She met her husband George Zaharias while golfing. He was a wrestler. They were married in 1938. George began to manage Babe's career. She won many golf tournaments. At one point, she won 14 tournaments in a row.

In 1953, Zaharias had a cancer operation, but she still played sports. A year later, she won the National Women's Open and the Tam O'Shanter All-America golf tournaments. Two years later, she died at the age of 42. In 1950, sports writers named Babe Didrikson Zaharias the outstanding woman athlete of the first half of the twentieth century.